The True Way to Achieve Success

BY

AWUDU QUAN

The True Way to Achieve Success

Copyright © 2021 by Awudu Quan
Cover design and edits by Candace Paul

All rights reserved. No part of this publication may be reproduced, distributed, or transmitted in any form or by any means, including photocopying, recording, or other electronic or mechanical methods, without the prior written permission of the author, except in the case of brief quotations embodied in critical reviews and certain other noncommercial uses permitted by copyright law. For permission requests, write to the publisher addressed "Attention: Publisher" at the email address below.

ISBN: 978-1-7333675-9-2

Ordering Information:
Quantity sales. Special discounts are available on quantity purchases by churches, associations, and others. For details, contact the author at the address below.
Orders by U.S. trade bookstores and wholesalers. Please email admin@aknowingspirit.com.

Dedication

To *my mentor, Denis Antoine.*
Thank you for all your support throughout the years and
for being a model of success that helped me find my path.

Preface

Since Adam, right up till now, scholars from various fields of study and walks of life have written countless books about success and how it can be achieved. Presumably, at any given moment, there are motivational speakers by the thousands lecturing on this topic. Better yet, I suspect, if you were to venture into a library there would be curious readers searching bookshelves and websites hoping to understand the concept of success, what it means, and exactly how to attain it.

Why? Well, it's simple…everybody wants to be successful in life. Nonetheless, the majority have not been able to make their dreams, their reality.

Does that mean there is something lacking in the array of books or endless hours of lectures about success? Not necessarily. But, I do believe that there is a *true* way to achieve success - specifically in terms of building wealth that can open the door to other possibilities.

There are indeed a few foundational principles that ring true for all successful people.

This book shall teach you.

CHAPTER 1
Introduction

When we say "success" what exactly do we mean? Most dictionaries define success as, "The attainment of wealth, position, honors, or the like." While success can of course be measured in many ways, this book will focus primarily on the attainment of wealth as the entry point to a successful life. So, how can one amass wealth?

Well, the definition given by the dictionary is very simple and straightforward when you know the true way. Conversely, without the true way, one can never achieve success.

Don't worry - you haven't missed out. If you are reading this book now, that means you are very lucky. You will soon discover how to attract success. I humbly recommend that you strictly practice whatever you read from this book and your desire to become successful will happen.

After reading this book, your life will never be the same. Unless you have settled on being unsuccessful, this book will certainly have an impact.

It is my sincere hope that you consider this work and apply it to your life.

There was a time in my life when I was seriously searching for ways to create wealth, but could not figure them out. The "true way" I'm about to share with you, helped me escape the heavy burden of poverty that became an Albatross around my neck.

To begin, often we see people moving all around the cardinal points feverishly seeking wealth. Many times this effort does not end well. Some have gone to prison, others lose their faith, and some even lose their life in the unfettered pursuit of wealth. Then there are others that do not have those tragic outcomes, but still never attain the success they hoped for. Sadly, many die in poverty without achieving the successful life they desired.

It is said that, "To have money is not a respecter of any religious belief." The intention of this book is not to condemn anyone's faith or beliefs, but to put things right for those willing to achieve success.

My people perish for lack of knowledge, are true words taken directly from the book of Hosea in the Holy Bible. The discussion above describes the consequences that often accompany a lack of knowledge. Unfortunately, those are the outcomes many people will experience. Many do not understand what true knowledge entails and thus will perish attempting to achieve success because they lack understanding.

There are fundamental principles and knowledge that one must acquire to become wealthy. This book teaches the fundamentals. Furthermore, as you continue to read and learn the true way to success, these discoveries may free you from poverty.

The funny thing is, everybody wants success. And although no one is born to fail, the truth remains that not everyone will be successful.

Nevertheless, those that normally succeed are also those who discover the true way to success and live by it. Success goes to those who walk to it. It is not difficult to achieve it, if only you know the true way. Going to and fro without understanding, won't get you there.

Now, whenever I see people not attaining the success they have sought; I simply see people without knowledge about the true way to achieve success. I believe that if you have read about successful people or listened to world-renowned motivational speakers, but you are still not successful in your own right, you just didn't come across the true way.

If this sounds familiar, do not worry. This book has come to redeem your situation.

CHAPTER 2
What You Need to Know

When I see people complaining of having no money, simultaneously I see people without specific skills and knowledge to generate money.

Money does not magically grow on trees free for the taking. Money goes to those who can generate it, or attract it. So, how can you become one of the people that generates or attracts money?

First, you must have vision. Buddha once said, "We are shaped by our thoughts. We become what think. When the mind is pure, joy follows like a shadow that never leaves."

Step one to being successful is to have a clear thought of who you want to become. This is the beginning of the true way to achieve success.

Plato, arguably one of the world's greatest thinkers and visionaries, once said, "The beginning is the most important part of the work." Ironically, most who claim to have vision, actually have none because they never start. If there is no beginning, there can be no middle or end.

How strong is your vision? I find people settle on anything as their vision - mainly because they have seen other people succeed on a particular path. But, that is where *your* vision becomes weak. Do not behave like a chicken that always follows the

the many directions of the wind without a specific achievable goal. Do not just follow the crowd. In choosing who you want to become, you must critically consider *your* strengths, *your* environment, and the availability of resources at *your* disposal to make your vision an eventual reality.

The most successful people who have ever lived and the ones you know today, are no different from you. Probably the only difference is that they critically observed and chose a vision that they could accomplish.

Once you are able to critically analyze and are able to choose a vision that you can accomplish, your focus, in the beginning, should not be on making money immediately. Instead, you should focus on how to make your chosen vision achievable. Ultimately, money is an end product of success. It will come.

Your vision must be *your* direction. If you do not know where you are going you will probably end up somewhere you do not really want to be. Therefore, you must really think about the things you want to do in life, and always administer your ways to suit your chosen vision.

Does your chosen vision align with what you truly want in life? The answer must be "yes" because this brings passion.

The conqueror, Napoleon Bonaparte, said, "Great ambition is the passion of a great character.

Those endowed with it may perform very good or very bad acts. All depends on the principles which direct them," said Bonaparte.

This quote shows that our attitude is our passion, and our passion becomes our vision. It is all one and the same. You must, therefore, develop your attitude about who you want to become. Set guiding principles and direction for yourself toward achieving your vision - especially, if the vision you choose has already been accomplished by someone else.

It is highly probable that you are not the first to have your vision. One of the truest statements written is that, "History is a repetition of itself." Whatever happens, more than likely has happened before. That means that we must learn from our predecessors. Nevertheless, we should blend it with our own style.

Embracing the qualities that make you unique will help produce the outcome that best suits you. That way you can make adjustments, use what works, while keeping your personal style.

CHAPTER 3
What You Need to Do:
Quotes to Live By

"There are basically two types of people. People who accomplish things, and people who claim to have accomplished things. The first group is less crowded." - Mark Twain

Having achievable goals does not mean that challenges will not come your way. "There is no tree that the wind has not shaken." In other words, challenges are part of every human experience.

Anthony Robbins, popular business strategist and life couch, once said: "The challenges that you go through to achieve your goals are not problems, but how you handle them makes them problems." In Robbins eyes, every problem was a gift because every problem was an opportunity to grow. For instance, challenges bring forth fear of failure. That's when you can combat fear with courage.

Coleman Young, believed that courage and fear were not far from each other. In fact, "Courage is one step ahead of fear," Young said. Walt Disney, whose first cartoon business went completely bankrupt, realized the pursuit is what matters. That failure led him to California - where after several failed attempts at acting, he decided to start an animation studio with his brother. That was the pursuit that worked!

Disney's famous quote: "All our dreams can come true, if we have the courage to pursue them," proved true in his own life.

So, how do we become courageous? You can only be courageous by persevering in patience and consistency. The Quran chapter 3 verse 200 speaks of this, "O ye who believe! Persevere in patience and constancy; vie in such perseverance; strengthen each other, and fear Allah that ye may prosper."

Do not opt for any quick decision to quit. Once you do, you become a failure.

"Success isn't always about greatness. It's about consistency. Consistent hard work leads to success. Greatness will come." This quote by Dwayne Johnson makes sense and we can see how it applied in his own life. Dwayne Johnson went from college football, to professional wrestler, then onto an acclaimed acting career.

Consistency honors good results. Khloe Kardashian, reality TV star and serial entrepreneur, had similar thoughts about consistency. "We all have to start somewhere, and doing something is better than nothing at all. Start small so you don't get discouraged and give up. Remember it is all about consistency."

This is typically the biggest reason why people quit, and you might experience it too. Your vision may not seem clear in the beginning, because you may not see any returns in the first few months after you start. This is the hardest part. This is also why so many never turn their dreams into their reality. They simply quit too soon.

During this period of no growth or tangible returns, you may even lose support from some of your family and friends. Some will classify you as a person who isn't serious. They may even go as far as to call you all sorts of names, but you must never be discouraged. Instead, continue to push forward with your vision until it comes true.

"Pain is temporary. Quitting lasts forever." said Lance Armstrong, former professional triathlete and cancer survivor. It is also said that, "You can't know how it feels to be blind if you are not blind yourself." The same way, no one can truly understand you, because every person is born with special qualities. This demonstrates that each person is born with unique abilities. This is why you should never quit because of someone's untoward comments regarding who you are.

Gradually, the change you desire will happen when you have put in enough effort and time. Once the change happens you will surprise and impress yourself. Moreover, that sense of accomplishment will help you press forward.

My father used to say: "It's never too late to do anything you wanted to do." Similarly, the great professional basketball player, Michael Jordan, acknowledged that, "You never know what you can accomplish until you try."

The path toward success is never easy. Steve Maraboli, a U.S. Air Force Veteran and acclaimed writer said: "Happiness is not the absence of problems; it's the ability to deal with them."

This is why you should devise a pragmatic approach to stay on track no matter how hardships, distractions, and unfortunate circumstances in life come your way. Keep going and develop a winner's mindset that at all cost you will succeed. It is just a matter of time.

Do not be bothered that those you started with have become successful, but you are not. "It does not matter how slowly you go as long as you do not stop," Confucius said. Never give up because your success is delayed. Jean de La Fontaine, famed fableist whose works are now considered masterpieces, once said, "There is no road of flowers leading to glory."

There is a strong correlation between success and patience. "Sometimes problems don't require a solution to solve them; instead they require maturity to outgrow them," Steve Maraboli said. Albert Einstein, Theoretical Physicist and one of the greatest thinkers to have lived, acknowledged that his success wasn't necessarily about smarts, but rather patience. "It's not that I'm so smart, it's just that I stay with problems longer," Einstein said.

The hidden truth about life is that the more challenges you face the stronger you become. You will also find that you develop charm and wit as you learn how to navigate challenges. Learn sooner rather than later the difference between "rest" and "quit". You rest when you are tired, you quit when you give up. Successful people don't quit.

You cannot persevere without self-discipline. "In reading the lives of great men, I found that the first victory they won was over themselves... self-discipline with all of them came first," This is a famous quote from the 33rd President of the United States, Harry S. Truman.

Self-discipline helps us win the victory over ourselves - over self-doubt, fear, laziness, and the like. You should, therefore, be self-disciplined because without self-discipline, you cannot realize your full potential.

"We need to steer clear of this poverty of ambition, where people want to drive fancy cars and wear nice clothes and live in nice apartments but don't want to work hard to accomplish these things. Everyone should try to realize their full potential," said Barak Obama First African-American President of the United States.

The bottom line is that all those who have rightfully earned their success, understand the value of self-discipline. Once you instill self-discipline into your daily routine, it will enable you to move forward by overcoming any obstacle that will step in your way. It help you hold on to your vision. You should know that to become who you want to be in life the meal is not already prepared, and you have been invited to dine. In life, you are the cook! You are the one planning the meal, adding the ingredients, and waiting for the finished product. This is why you must be self-disciplined in all aspects, in order to cook the best food you want for your life. This also means that you must avoid the common behaviors among those who consistently fail such as: Procrastination, believing falsely that some people are born NOT to succeed, lack of self-trust, and lack of inner strength among others. These beliefs will hinder you from achieving your dreams.

CHAPTER 4
What You Need to Check

As I indicated in the introduction, you must consider your environment when choosing who you want to become. Your chosen environment must support your success. So what is your environment? In this context, your environment is your circle of friends and business associates. We have all heard that "birds of a feather flock together." This means that like-minded people move together. Therefore, on your road to success, you should always surround yourself with like-minded people. Eventually, this choice cultivates teamwork.

Patrick Lencioni, writer and business management expert, called teamwork "A strategic decision." You should identify people with the same interests and work together. Brian Tracy, a Canadian born motivational speaker says, "Teamwork is so important that it is virtually impossible for you to reach the heights of your capabilities or make the money that you want without becoming very good at it."

The mistake many people make is that they have a great vision but select the wrong environment - friends and business associates. As a result, they are not able to carry the vision forward.

For instance, a football game and a swim meet do not happen in the same place. They are two entirely different games. This is applicable to life.

First, you should not involve yourself with any activity which antagonizes your vision. Second, you should exempt yourself from naysayers. If you fail to do these two important things, you won't go far. Furthermore, the vision you had for your life will not become a reality.

As previously mentioned, self-discipline brings about self-confidence. And self-confidence will help you make the necessary changes that will energize and prompt you to be positive and productive every single day. Your daily communication should be with those with similar goals and ambitions as yours. Take the time to read more about successful people who had visions similar to yours - learn their stories, their failings, and their triumphs.

Still, most important is continually developing who you want to become. Once you have the right mindset, then you have all the reasons you need to ignore the negative people and all the things that will divide your attention from achieving your vision. We have often heard the phrase, "One's network determines his *next* work or wealth."

If this is true, you must surround yourself with positive-minded people. People who have succeeded in your chosen vision. Those who you can discuss ideas with, in addition to offering meaningful support.

It is also important to learn from your mistakes. That is the only way to constantly check yourself and re-evaluate your strategy.

We've often heard that, "The downfall of a man is not the end of his life." However, it's common to see the downfall becoming - for the the majority of people, the end of their lives.

The only way one can recognize that the downfall is not the end, is to learn from those mistakes. The first step to success is failure.

The times you fail do not matter, what matters is to learn from what made you fail, and build upon that knowledge in order to succeed next time. Learning from your mistakes will truly help you understand what things are important. For example, you don't learn to train as a footballer when in fact, your aim is to become a renowned boxer and vice versa. Stay focused on who you want to become continue to increase your burning desire to succeed.

Once again, your attitude forms the basis of your habits. Your habits are the actions that are regularly done. With this in mind, you must develop good habits - that will help you become successful. This means that all your good habits should be implemented everyday toward the outcome you want. Consider each day a new beginning. The "new beginning" in this context is not starting something different every day, but rather learning something new related to your goal. When you do this you will not be far from achieving success in your life.

CHAPTER 5
What You Need to Manage

In this chapter you will learn about time management. Poet and retired professor, Tom Greening said, "All time management begins with planning." There is no doubt that effective time management is the key to success. You must be what I like to call "self-time" conscious. People tend to see time management as managing the time. It's not. It is about changing and managing your own behaviors which waste time. Charles Darwin, scientist who devised the theory of evolution, had a unique understanding of time. "A man who dares to waste one hour of time has not discovered the value of life."

In the same vain, martial artist and Kung-fu legend, Bruce Lee stated: "If you love life, don't waste time, for time is what life is made up of. Everybody has 24 hours each day. You can increase your wealth when you manage yourself effectively but cannot extend your time. "Where your attention goes, your time goes," said Idowu Koyenikan, internationally acclaimed organizational consultant and author.

Paul J. Meyer is considered by many to be a leader in the self-improvement industry. His programs and books have sold more than two billion dollars worldwide. He believed productivity was a conscious decision. "Productivity is never an accident. It is always the result of a commitment to excellence, intelligent planning, and focused effort," Meyer said.

This is why you should be self-conscious about all you do since productivity is never an accident. Martin Luther King, Jr. who led the the fight for civil rights even said, "We must use time creatively."

One secret about life is that the past becomes the present-moment, the present-moment becomes the future. Buddha said, "Do not dwell in the past, do not dream of the future, concentrate the mind on the present moment."

It goes without saying that the effort you put in the present-moment becomes your future. Therefore, do not waste your present time thinking about the past, rather use it judiciously to do something meaningful about who you want to be in the future. The future is not found in the past. "The time for action is now. It's never too late to do something," said Antoine de Saint-Exupery, French poet, writer, and aviator.

How can you become self-time conscious? You can only become self-time conscious when you begin to realize that time is life, and therefore, every minute of time spent must be given to how you envision your life. Once you are able to recognize this truth, the importance of managing yourself effectively every single day to achieve your life goals will be your priority.

The following guidance should be critically administered. They are as follows:

1. *Set goals*. Within each goal, write down specific things you need to do.
2. *Rank your goals*. Here, scale them in order of priority and preference. The most pressing goal should be first.
3. *Prepare*. This is your plan. This very important step will help you to get things done effectively - and not harp on unimportant tasks.
4. *Stay away from all distractions.* Avoid all that distracts you. Have the courage to say no to unimportant things.
5. *Review goals daily.* This way you can always check if you are on schedule, meeting deadlines, and obligations.

CHAPTER 6
YOUR SUCCESS IS HERE

It is my prayer that just as you have read this book, your dreams and aspirations come true. I am confident that if you put all that you have read here into practice, your life will never be the same. There are those who will only read this book, but will not bother to practice what book is about. I hope you are not one of them!

In short, you must have a vision and pursue your vision. Life will present many challenges during this pursuit, but you must not quit - instead, you must persevere and be patient. This is because consistency brings a successful result.

Once you quit, you become a failure. Winners don't quit…they rest. You must choose the right environment by surrounding yourself with like-minded people. This will boost your confidence. Finally, you must manage your time properly. Time is money. Everybody has 24 hours each day. Manage them wisely. Those who manage their days well become successful. You can be one of them.

This is the true way to achieve success!

Aknowledegments

First, glory be to God for my life. I also wish to acknowledge, with unique thanks, the assistance of those who have helpfully provided their time and support making this publication achievable, with special mention of my parents Nana Zacharia Appiah (Father), Abenaa Fati Yeboah (Mother), my wife Chen Wen and my daughter Yebuwa Kuan for their inspiration.

My special gratitude is extended to Mr. Kwadwo Ntim Atuahene for his support. Mr kwadwo Ntim Atuahene is a retired Civil Servant. He worked for about thirty (30) years. Positions he held included Minister (Trade and Investment) Ghana Mission, Beijing, Director, Domestic Trade (Ministry of Trade and Industry), Chief Executive, Ghana Free Zones Board, and Deputy Administrator, GetFund, Ghana. Mr. Atuahene holds MSc (econ planning), LLM (Petroleum Law and Policy), Solicitor and Barrister at Law (Supreme Court of Ghana), BA (Russian Language), Diploma, trade Law (WTO), and Diploma (French Language).

Also, special thanks are extended to Mr. John Mensah Apreban for his encouragement. Mr. John Mensah Apreban holds master's degree in Law and Development from the University of Cape Coast and B.A Hons. from the University of Ghana. He works as a Principal Administrator at the National Human Rights Institution of Ghana (Commission on Human Rights and Administrative Justice). He is a human rights defender and believes in equity.

I further acknowledge H.E. Dr. Denis G. Antoine for his review, comments, and recommendation for the improvement of this work.

H.E. Dr. Denis G. Antoine is the former Ambassador Extraordinary and Plenipotentiary of Grenada to the People's Republic of China from January 2016-2019. His functions included the full responsibilities for maintaining effective bilateral diplomatic relationship between the PRC and Grenada; and promotion of his country's interest within the community of nations represented in China and neighboring countries.

He is the Former Ambassador/Permanent Representative of Grenada to the United Nations from 2013 to 2015. Ambassador Antoine was elected and served as Vice President of the United Nations General Assembly for the 69th Session.

Before being appointed to serve at United Nations, Ambassador Antoine was Ambassador-At-Large and Director of the Office of International Programs and Exchange at University of the District of Columbia in Washington, D.C from 2009 to 2013.

During his tenure at the University, the Ambassador engaged in the conduct of Education Diplomacy, which included leading high-level delegations to countries such as Thailand, India, Egypt, China, Nigeria, Liberia, Ghana, Equatorial Guinea, London, and Sunderland in The United Kingdom. He worked closely with the Embassies of the Golf States, and other diplomatic Missions in Washington, D.C to promote negotiate and sign cooperation agreements with institutions of higher education, and conduct educational seminars.

Ambassador Antoine has served as Senior Election Observer with the Organization of American States (OAS), on missions to Guyana, Jamaica, and Commonwealth Dominica.

When he demitted Office in 2009, he was the second highest-ranking ambassador to the United States in Washington D.C. As one of the longest-serving ambassadors for his country, H.E Denis G. Antoine served as Grenada's Ambassador to the United States of America and Permanent Representative to the Organization of American

States (OAS) in Washington, D.C and non-resident Ambassador for Grenada to Mexico and Panama concurrently, from 1995 to 2009.

He was Education Coordinator for Catholic Charities, Model Cities, in Washington, D.C from 1993-1994 and Education Supervisor for the District of Columbia Public Schools until 1995. Before his appointment as Ambassador of Grenada to the United States, Denis G. Antoine served as Program Specialist - Service Facility Regulator Department of Consumer and Regulatory Affairs for the Government of the District of Columbia from 1990 – 1992.

Ambassador Antoine has more than twenty (20) years of high level bilateral diplomatic experience in the United States, Mexico and Panama, the Inter-American System, and globally, which began when he served as Deputy Head of Mission and Counsellor/Alternate Representative to the OAS at the Embassy of Grenada in Washington, D.C, and as Charge d'Affairs during the period of May 1985 to December 1990.

He is the 2008 recipient of the Martin Luther King Jr. Legacy Award for International Service, he was the former Dean of the Corps of Ambassadors of the Western Hemisphere, and the Vice Dean of all ambassadors represented in the United States. He represented Grenada on the Board of Directors of the Inter-American Agency for Cooperation and Development (IACD) and served as Chairman of the Board of Directors of the Young Americas Business Trust, an affiliate of the OAS that works on youth and entrepreneurship in the Americas, and other charitable foundations.

Publications include "Get on Board Children of the World" 2020; "Effective Diplomacy in the Twenty-First Century: 2020; "Why is Everybody Looking at Me" in 2019 and a contribution to **UN-HABITAT CSU** Public Spaces for Sustainable Urbanization published by Talal Abu-Ghazaleh & Co. International in November 2016. In 2012, he published "Voice of Representation" a collection of letters, messages, and speeches of an ambassador and in 2009 he published a book "Effective Diplomacy – A Practitioners Guide" shares his insights on applied diplomacy in The United States of America and beyond.

About the Author

Awudu Quan, is the Chief Executive Officer of Beijing Mingyue Business Co., Ltd, and a managing partner of Quan Awudu Limited, and Maasikat Limited. Mr. Quan is a successful Ghanaian writer, entrepreneur, a businessman, and aspiring legal practitioner. Mr. Quan is the President of the Ghanaian Community Association in China, Beijing Chapter. In addition to this, Mr. Quan has initiated several programs to promote investment opportunities in Africa and the Caribbean.

www.ingramcontent.com/pod-product-compliance
Lightning Source LLC
Chambersburg PA
CBHW060413080526
44583CB00012B/561